RECOVERY

Copyright © 2020 Ishpreet Kaur Bhogal

All rights reserved.
No reproduction without permission.

Written and arranged by
Ishpreet Kaur Bhogal
@ishpreetwrites

Cover design © Satvir Sihota
@satvir.illustrations

ISBN: 9798602867398

RECOVERY

WRITTEN BY
ISHPREET KAUR BHOGAL

ILLUSTRATED BY
SATVIR SIHOTA

Written in memory of
Jaswinder Kaur Bhogal
1964-2018

CONTENTS

2013	13
2016	37
2018	61
2020	89

Mum this is for you,
it was all for you.

2013

Poetry for me has been a form of creative expression. Creating a story in four lines, sharing a memory in one and evoking emotion through a single word. Some show their power in action, mine lie in the words you read.

I'm not your conventional bookworm. I guess I found it difficult to relate to some of the stories I read when I was younger, it just didn't hit me the same way poetry did. I'd read one poem and think about it for weeks on end. I couldn't fathom how so much could be said, with such few words, until things changed at home.

2013 was the year it all changed for my family and I. My dad picked me up from school one day and didn't say anything the whole car journey. That was quite normal for us; we often would sit in comfortable silence listening to Desi-Radio, but something just didn't seem right that day. I just remember him turning into our road and hitting the curb, and I made a comment saying, 'what's happening?' He scratched the alloys again pulling into our drive. For a man that valued his new car, he sure didn't care anymore.

I only remembered as we got out the car, that mum had an appointment earlier that day. Just before opening the front door, he said to me, 'she'll be getting chemo'.

My dad and I share pretty much the same personality; we are both quiet individuals, happily keep to ourselves and are just pretty chilled humans. I'm the youngest but favourite child of the clan, (it's okay, they know). He's my best friend, and that very day was the first time I saw my best friend upset.

I had no clue what to say after dad told me. Walking into the house felt like I was walking into unknown territory.

I felt stuck in the porch, thinking, ok- do I just act like dad didn't just tell me or shall I just go give mum a hug, or pretend like it's all good. I had absolutely no clue.

I just followed dad inside and saw mum sunken in the sofa in tears, with my sisters trying to console her. I went with 'everything is going to be fine mum', meaningless words of support because I myself didn't know if she'd get better. I moved to another room and sat in silence with dad.

I guess my coping mechanism was research, being 15 and unaware of anything 'bad' was definitely a shock to the system. My parents never got ill, they weren't allowed to, they needed to look after us. But that day I saw a weakness in my father's eyes and tiredness in my mums, and I just couldn't bear it.

Being the youngest in my family, I felt that I had very little to offer in terms of support. I was still in school, and I was expected to continue as normal because mum didn't want my 'studies' to be affected. My teachers didn't know what was happening at home, I didn't want their pity, or to be seen differently. But school became hard for me. I couldn't concentrate as normal. I was always thinking about mum.

I'd be thinking about what to make for dinner that evening, the laundry that needed sorting, the prescription that I needed to collect, there was just so much going on in my head.

Soon it became normal because we've always known to work as a team. My sisters would take mum to her appointments, organise her medications and make sure everything was going according to her treatment plan.

I'd always try help in other ways and for some time, I was the listener. I knew consultations weren't easy, I just wish I knew what everything meant.

I just wished I were a doctor with 10 years of medical experience so I could have seen this coming.

RECOVERY

I wished to take your **pain**,
to see you not.

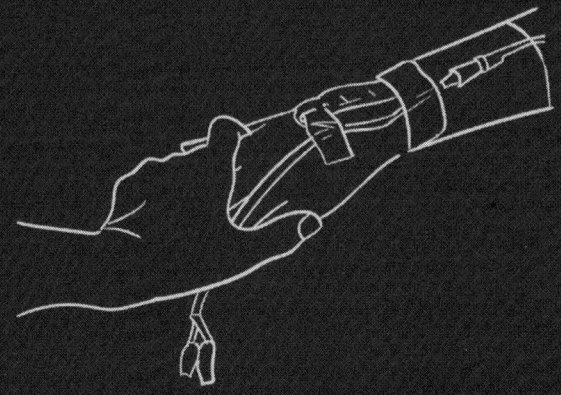

My morning routine

I wake up, not hearing my alarm
One minute early, I wait to turn it off.
Lying in bed
I hear my dad enter, just before 7.

Mums awake, I hear her moving.
The sound of her harsh vomit
Crowds the noise of the aeroplanes.
The toilet flushes, to drain her emptiness.
Wipes come out, to clean the evidence.

But I know.

Tears form in the corner of her eyes,
Back stretched.
She brushes her teeth like normal,
Mouthwash gargled.
Face wiped, smile applied.

I roll out of bed, and say
Good morning mum.

Speak to me

I usually start the conversation,
But I'll let her speak.
My ears are yours,
And so is my time.

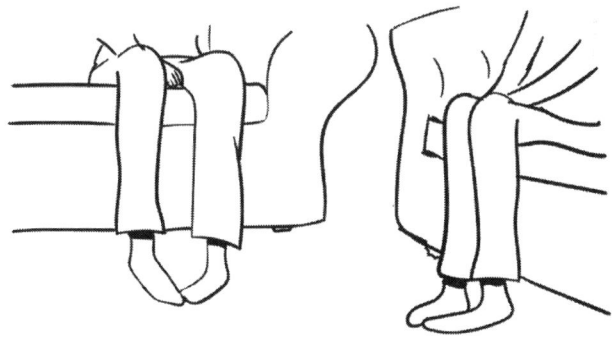

Last one standing

Go to sleep.
I'll stay up and care for you,
I'm your security.

Medication

Domperidone- anti sickness
Bendroflumethiazide- high blood pressure
Metoclopramide- anti sickness
Omeprazole- settles the stomach
Losartan potassium- high blood pressure control
Apixaban- blood circulation
Diazepam- for sleepless nights
Paclitaxecel- the cancer drug
Dexamethasone- steroid
Zometa- bone strength
Calcium- bone strength
Sando k- potassium's
Tinzaparin- injection
Clarithomyicin- antibiotics
Capecitobin- the new cancer drug

'You should feel better now'

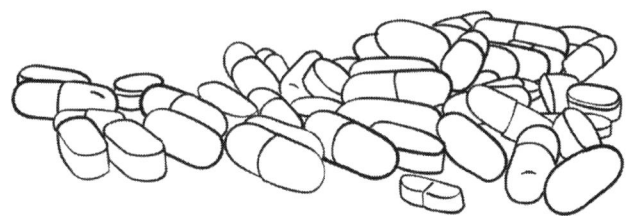

Side effects

Her power weakened those not worthy,
Her hair, her nails, her insecurities.

Repeat

If I could rewind certain memories
As I do with my music playlist,
I'd still feel played.

Life expectancy

Tears stream from mums face
When she hears her chemo will stop.
Dad tries to console her,
He just woke up.

I sit, eyes fixated to the floor.
I have nothing to say.
I have no tears to shed.
Emotions locked.

I don't know how long you'll be with me,
But I want you to say you'll stay.

So please, as naïve it is to say,
Don't leave.

Come closer

I need you to pick me up,
And hold me tight.
Let me rest
My overworked mind
On your lap.

Whilst you stroke my head,
And tell me
To put oil in my hair.

Need

Sleepless nights.
Obscured days.
Blurred images.
Hazy.

I need your warmth to comfort me.

Hands together

My prayers
Answered or unanswered,
I'm not sure
What I wanted.

I need a hug

I like hugs.
It's an excuse for me
To let go
Of everything inside,
And fall into the person holding me.
For those brief seconds
I'm calm and content.
Till I let go,
And feel all alone again.

A fathers hand

When I lie on the sofa
Tired from battling a long day.
You place your hand on my forehead,
With a soft pressure.
For those brief moments,
I feel a release from my stress,
Because you take them all away.

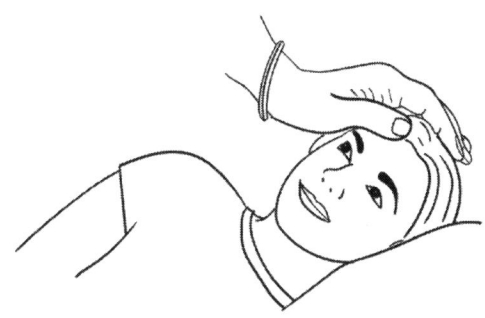

Love

You twisted and turned
In all situations,
Uncomfortable.
So your children
Could rest.

Reflection

Time for bed, we make our way upstairs.
The *ramal* mum ties, slowly unties.
She sits at the edge of her bed.
Stares at the mirror in front of her
With disgust.
Pigmented dark patches on her face.
Tired eyes.
Hairless head.

'What is this life', so she says
I stand frozen, unable to forge the right words,
Sit next to her and say

'My life is great, because you are in it'

Hard as a **nail** but soft as **butter**.
- Dad's character reference of mum

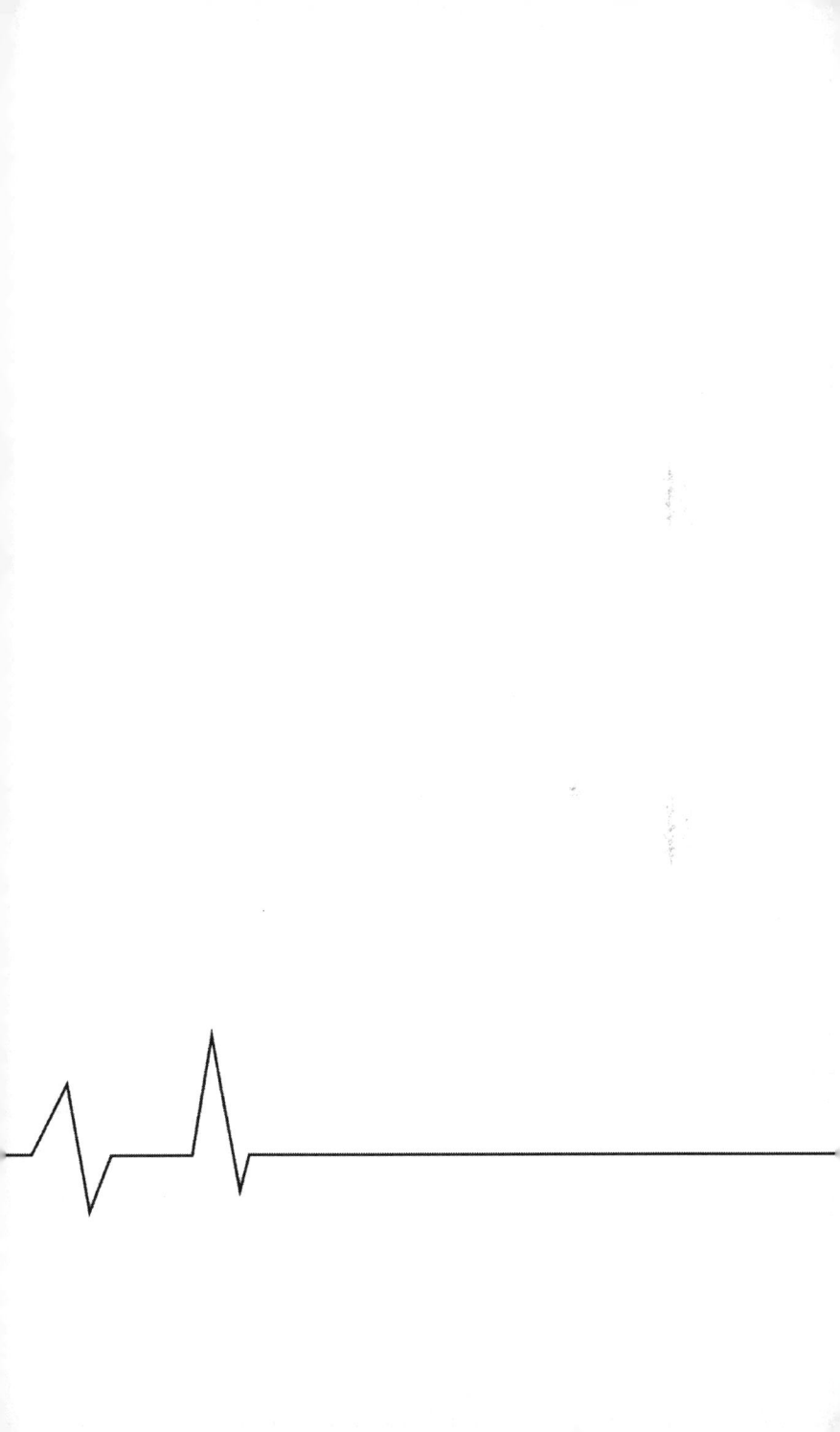

2016

The next few years, definitely became a rollercoaster ride. Mum had all her treatments, chemo and radiotherapy, the whole works. We even thought that after everything, she was in the clear. But that lasted maybe a year until it came back again and came back worse.

Our last big family holiday was in 2016; it was the last time we went to India as a four and unfortunately the last time my mum's sisters saw her. I think we all did a lot of growing up following 2016. I had just started university, everything was all still new for me, and I was playing catch up with life. I'm really lucky to have some friends that I can call family, as each consultation at the hospital usually lead to a meltdown at uni.

I was mums release. I sat with her, listened to her and shared her pain. I will never be able to fully understand everything she felt, but I tried. It was hard. It *is* hard seeing your parent cry. It's hard being the one wiping their tears. My heart sinks to the thought of it, but we were partners.

The family calendar was specifically for mum. It kept us all up to date with mum's appointments, which meant that she never had to go alone. We made sure of it. My sisters would book time off, I'd miss university some days and my dad would, at times, book weeks off during mums' treatments and recovery. We were lucky we could share the responsibility, and everyone did.

I remember sitting in a hospital room with mum waiting for the nurses to come back to explain why she was getting really bad headaches. We were both feeling so anxious and nauseous about what they may say. I never held her hand so tight, before that day.

I was listening to the nurses and doctors talk outside, discussing how they should tell us, the 'news'. I just knew it. I knew it but I didn't want to be right. I could feel mum's heart racing in my hand. And I knew what she feared.

Once mum was re-diagnosed, we were constantly on the move. There was no rest period. The next two years went by so quickly; we didn't have a chance to take a breather. Family conference calls became a regular thing, so we all knew what was going on. Mum had a full itinerary and although most of it was jumping from hospital to hospital, it kept her busy. She kept me busy.

I kept a brave face for a very long time, maybe a little too long, because I didn't quite know how to adjust emotionally to all the changes we made to our lifestyle. I guess my non-existent emotions at the time were handy during consultations. I was often mistaken for a junior doctor on many occasions, because I'd walk around with a folder full of mum's notes. This was useful when interrogating professional and well-qualified consultants.

We were working with borrowed time, and my sisters and I made sure to extend it for as long as possible. We did our best to protect mum, to keep her from dinner table talk, misheard conversations and gossip.

I grew at times very bitter when put in situations where I had to smile perfectly and converse nicely. All these unfamiliar faces grew my frustrations, and I just wanted to keep mum in bubble wrap, packed tight away from harm.

Voices travelled and so did uninvited assumptions. But we were a strong unit. Dad always managed to brush off negativity, so effortlessly. His only job was to annoy mum, and he did that perfectly.

RECOVERY

I'm almost so **okay** being by myself,
I'm beginning to **hurt** others.

What I claim

I am fine.
Struggling to pick up
Fragments of my heart,
Scattered like broken glass.

Dirt on my fingers,
So easily rubbed off,
Like my emotions.

Flickered lights,
Blinking from inside.

I am broken.
But I am fine.

Unfamiliar faces

You stroke my arm
As if *you'll* console me.
Words are repeated
Slowly and calmly,
As if *I'll* break.

You pity me,
Then judge when you walk away.
I don't like you.

Formality calls

The telephone rings quite often in this house.
'Is your mum there?'
Reassurance is what others seek,
Not often thinking what she needs.

'I didn't see you at that last event,
Is everything alright'
Quick to pass judgments,
'Stay positive'.

Your meaningless words hold dishonesty,
I don't need your formality calls.

A **broken** vase glued back together, will still show each **mended** crack.

Attendance

Attendance is mandatory when invitations are sent.
Expectations are set prior to attendance.
Opinions are formed without our consent.
Misheard stories are the first to attend.

When we walk in,
Pity and fake sympathy
Attract like magnets.

I paint confidence on my face,
Fight comments like battles
And burn them with the rage
Fuelled in my body.

You ask for our attendance,
Yet you question why we are here.

Weather change

It's 10 degrees.
It's 32 degrees.
It's 38 degrees.
It's 20 degrees.
It's 8 degrees.

Constantly adjusting to environments
That do not suit me.
Constantly adjusting to changes,
I did not see coming.

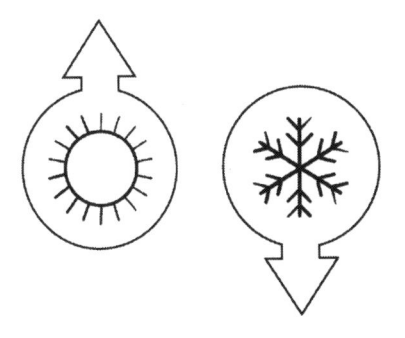

Wisdom tooth

Numb.
Delicate to touch.
Constant dull ache.

Realness comes like a toothache.

One day at a time

Each day comes like waves.
I never know when
I'll be above water,
Or drowning in my emotions.

It's a never-ending race, where I'm **running** for more time with you.

Sunrise

At times,
Everyday.
I'd wake up
With a wet pillow.

Pain relief

Hold on to the pain
Grab it tight.
After a while,
You won't realise
It gave you relief.

Imbalance

I never knew
What was going to happen.
But I held your hand,
And that was enough
To keep my heart
Intact.

I'm yours

I'll be your legs, when you can't walk.
I'll be your mind, when you can't think straight.
I'll hold you up, when you fall into me.
I'll care for you, like you do for me.

I'll smile, and hope that it reaches your heart.
I'll make you laugh, so you forget the past.
I'll let you speak, whilst I listen.
I'll sit right next to you, to keep you company.

Your food reaches my stomach.
Your happiness is my strength.
Your guidance puts me in gear.
Your battle is my battle.

I will always be here for you, each and everyday.
But right now, I need you to be *here* for me.

You pulled me close,
how a **flower** turns
to the **sun**.

Footsteps

You carried such power that
Your every movement,
Turned an expression
The whole room,
Managed
To move with you.

2018

Mum passed away on Sunday 16th September 2018. This has been, by far, the hardest day of my life. I've lost both sets of grandparents, and I thought my quota was met for the number of people I had lost, but clearly not. I remember the day so vividly it still makes me nauseous.

The weeks mum was in hospital were so painfully draining. I was off work for a month, my sisters took emergency leave and dad literally lived at the hospital. We'd drive in the morning, and stay there till late at night. Dinners were often at 10pm or non-existent.

We'd be snacking throughout the day; everyone's routine went out the window. We turned mums hospital room into a gym, an office and an entertainment area. We spoke about everything in the future, everything she had to look forward to. I wasn't sure if it was false hope, maybe it was a hope we needed to keep as a family, but it was a hope that my dad kept till her last breath.

I think I was angry for a whole year. I've never felt so bitter, hurt and angered before and I just wanted the pain to stop. I needed to stop the hurting but I didn't know what to do, how to heal a broken wound that wouldn't be repaired the same way, they usually do. My health wasn't good. I comfort ate a lot, gained a lot of weight and grew stiff and miserable. I'd lounge on the sofa and on the bed all day. I was sick, for a very long time. Loss really hurts. No one can explain the gut wrenching feeling in your heart, no one can prepare you, but all I can say, is that it bloody hurts.

I found it very hard talking about mum to my own family. For the first six months I couldn't look at her picture, because I was angry and hurt.

I'd try communicating with my sisters but tears would constantly stream on my face. I didn't know I could be so angry.

I didn't know whom I was angry with but I questioned my religiosity. I felt as though I had been tested and challenged for six consecutive years, and I still lost in the end.

I kept thinking, 'why, why have we as a family been put in this situation?' I was tired of feeling so lost and incomplete. I just needed her to come back and put me back together again.

I still need her.

'On Sunday 9th June 2019, Daddy Ji woke up and decided we were going to the Gurdwara today. It was like he woke up with such conviction and demanded that we go. So we did. When I was sitting upstairs in the darbar (prayer) hall I couldn't quite shake the sadness I felt in my heart. I just couldn't breathe, hunched over with my hands tangled together. The one place where you'd find the most peace brought such heaviness in my heart, that I proceeded to have an anxiety attack. I just sat there, whilst the kirtan (religious hymns) was running symphonies in the back of my mind, crying. Tissues built in my lap with my sister's arms around me. Nothing was said, nothing changed- we just sat together and cried.'
- Excerpt from my letters

RECOVERY

Your mum made me the **richest** man.
- Dad

I Phone

Storage reached to full capacity.
Personal issues removed like apps,
They take up too much space.

Download our memories on to a hardrive.
Buy some time, with iCloud.
Monthly payments made to make space,
For the adventures that are yet to take place.

Upgrade notified every month,
Till, my phone wears out over time.
Updates to my phone take longer to respond,
To the new fixes and bugs that are on my phone.

So slowly, the device operates.
Screen brightness reduced to optimize battery life.
Eyes worn out by the hope it survives.

Till the black screen faces my bare skin,
It can no longer be re-charged.

It's gone.

Home becomes house

Every weekend since,
Regular visits,
Re-visits the same conversation.
Re-visits the same role I take in the kitchen.

Whilst you imprint your position in my house,
I'm the one trying to escape.

I want to be here

Sometimes I just want to come home
And be at home.
But I struggle to find peace,
Within these walls my parents built together.

And right now,
It doesn't feel like home.

Tea time

Your comments spill out
Like a split tea bag.
Brewing on the gas
Changes my colour,
Boils the heat within me.

Whilst you sieve out all my broken fragments,
And sip on my pain,

I offer you biscuits.

Absors- **Punjabi word 'to pay your respects'**

By coming to my house and sitting for 3 hours,
Benefits your self-esteem knowing
You spent time with us.
But whilst you were having your tea
Speaking of my mother so fondly,
I was hiding, trying to get space.
From your constant re-assurance,
That this is all going to be ok.

Despite your in-frequent attendance
And concern when she was here.

Tears: on demand face wash

Heartbroken

Who knew that dealing with heartbreak
Would literally break you.
I'm torn because the one person
That knows how to fix everything and anything,
Was the person who caused my heartbreak.

My heart hurts

Tightness in my chest.
Stiffness in neck.
Breathless.
Clenched stomach.
Heavy head.
Tired.

Months have passed since you left,
But my heart still aches your presence.

DNR

She said no to CPR
And there was nothing I could say.

Her body, her pain
Our loss.

I can't do this

I can't do this,
I genuinely can't.

I'm tired of people's regular visits.
I'm tired of the small talk.
I'm tired of pretending that I'm ok
Because I know that I'm not.

I'm tired of the pain,
I just want it to stop.

Chest pain

My chest aches,
You've left me
And I'm scared.

Lost

Places became familiar.
Your pain became familiar.
Our journeys became familiar.
My role became familiar.

Now I'm just lost without you.

Can't

Some religious hymns bring more pain than comfort.
It brings me back to the time,
When we were praying in your hospital room.

Dry eyes

There will come a time when I stop crying,
I just don't know when that will be.

Till then, pass me something
That will soak up
A bathtub full of emotions,
That's about to flood our house.

Is it you or me

I'd tear up, but your cheeks would be wet.
You'd be in pain, but I'd bleed.
My skin would peel, to your medication.
Your mind would block, so I'd listen.

Together our hearts broke.

When you saw tears run down, my cheeks.
When I could not stop the pain
And no longer cream your blistered feet.

Now that you've left,
My whole is incomplete.

Sunken

I melted into
My bed sheets.
Sought comfort into,
The pillowcases
That muted my cry.

I hide my **heartbreak** with a **smile**, it's as if nothing ever happened.

Hiding

My skin aches for your embrace.
My heart longs for your love.
My hair falls for your touch.
My mind collects your words.

My eyes sore, searching for you.

I was not big enough to hold you

Only once,
I carried your whole weight.

Your arms wrapped around
My whole body.
Your legs collapsed
Inwards.
Your head sunken
On my shoulder.

Only once.
Could I carry
Your heartache,
Your pain,
Your burdens,
Your emotions,
Your tiredness,
Your whole being.

For those brief seconds,
I felt my shoulders, stiffen
My back, stretch
My heart, break.

Because I was not big enough,
To carry a mothers weight.

2020

'It's been over a year since you've left us but there are times it feels longer and times when I feel- I just lost you. When your photo was printed for the funeral, I couldn't bear to look at you. I hated the fact that you now come in a picture frame; I felt that I could no longer speak to you.

Only now do I look at your photo and say good morning. My day starts with you and ends with you. I hear your voice telling me to study, to stop watching tv and to go sleep when we've been up till late. I just need your voice to be a little louder sometimes, just a little louder.

-Excerpt from my letters 18/12/19

It took a lot of time and a lot of strength. I only confided in my family, and my friends have been my saviours. I know that during this whole grievance process, I have messed up a few relationships, whether personally or through family. I pushed a lot of people away, but the people who stayed and came back, were the individuals who strengthened me.

Over time I learnt how to carry my own voice again, I learnt how to smile and be at peace in my own solitude. I learnt that it was okay to feel what I felt, and what I still carry in my own heart. Everyone grieves differently and my transition and adjustment felt, at times, longer than the other members of my family.

My teenage/adulthood was very different to my sisters and I felt very lost after losing mum. I needed to find a new purpose for myself, because I no longer had someone relying on me. I really struggled finding peace. I sought comfort in people that didn't have the capacity to fill the love that mum gave, and I knew no one could replace her.

After a very long time, I found a new confidence in myself that I lost when mum became ill. I know I overshadowed my emotions and kept them hidden because I found them to be an 'inconvenience'. But over time, and with the help of counselling, I found better ways of dealing with the hurt and pain, one of which lead to writing.

I was so tired of seeing mum in pain that I just didn't express any of my emotions, because I knew it would only make her feel worse. I thought putting on a 'front' was 'practical' during consultations and doctors appointments, but it broke me inside.

You can feel sad, angry and frustrated with changes in your life. I still feel all those emotions, and I believe that's okay. I know mum was a very strong woman and I am strong now too, because of her. We lifted each other up.

A lot of time has passed, family dynamics have changed, my chest still pains and now, I'm the one recovering.

RECOVERY

My parents are like **salt** and **pepper**, they are not one without the other.

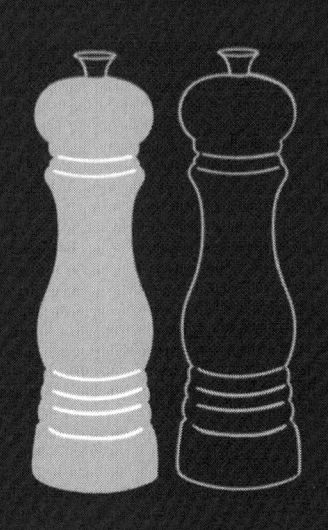

Delay

I wish your absence were affected by Indian timing.
But it was wrong for me to wish a delay,
For your pain.

It doesn't get any easier

Tachycardic heart rate.
Detached mind.
Limbless body.
Weakened eyes.

All I did was open her wardrobe.

Try

You have to let go.
Let go of the hurt.
Let go of the pain.
Let go.

Appreciate

Each day, be thankful.
Be grateful.

As we carried hope,
That she'd make it till tomorrow.

Take me back

Each reprimand.
Each disagreement.
Each lecture.
Each argument.

Brings more warmth then ever,
Now.

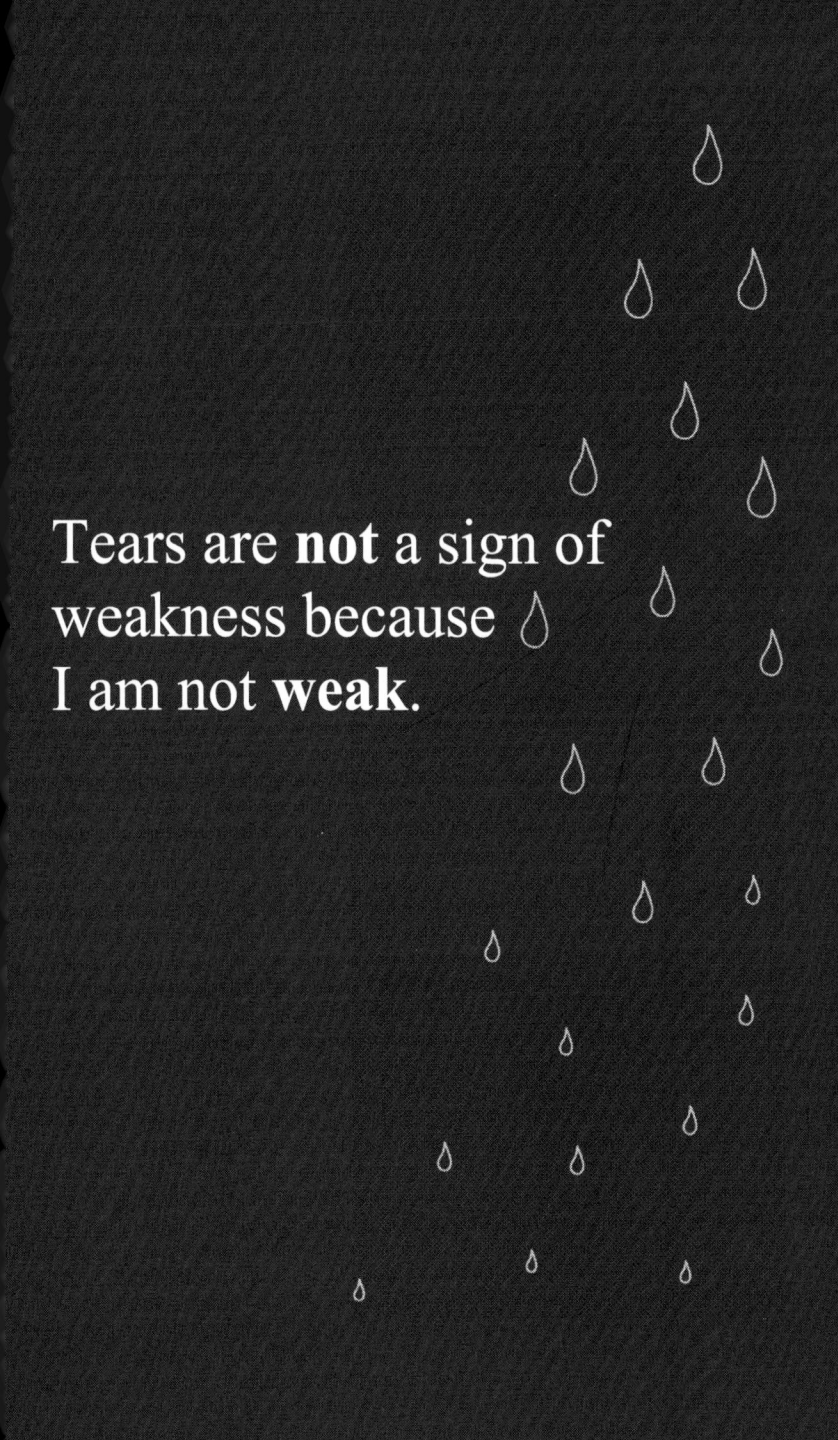

Tears are **not** a sign of weakness because I am not **weak**.

We share things differently now

Each failure, I long for your consolation.
Each tear, I long for your fingertips.
Each happiness, I long to share with you.
Each success, I long for your pride.

Now I just tell you everything
Through your picture frame.

You still take my pain away,
I just wipe my own tears.
My happiness comes from,
The joy you would have felt.

Each success for me,
Will forever be attaining your pride.

I'm a work in progress

I'm working on it.
I'm working on this.
I'm working on me.

Sound

We speak about you.
Share stories about you.
It feels weird,
These moments of laughter
And

I can't hear your voice.

Wake up

It's hard to stop thinking about,
Someone that's worth thinking about.
For endless hours, days and nights.

My thoughts create memories,
As if I make my dreams about you.
You become real,

It's almost as if I never lost you.

Aura

At family gatherings
I feel you.
Your warmth.
Your love.
Your protection.

Who knew true love existed

Soft eyes, gentle smile.
Relaxed shoulders,
Carefree.

There was no distance.
Nothing could keep your hearts,
Apart.

You held her hand.
Grabbed each fingertip,
And held her towards you.

Whilst she got lost in your gaze,
You managed to capture
All the moments,
She was falling in love with you.

Your touch left a **permanence** on all things **temporary**.

Story time

I shared my heart with you,
As you did with me.
Your expressions would make me,
A character in your story.

For I wish your story would go on,
For many more chapters.
So I could show you,
The story I've created for you.

Love you mum.

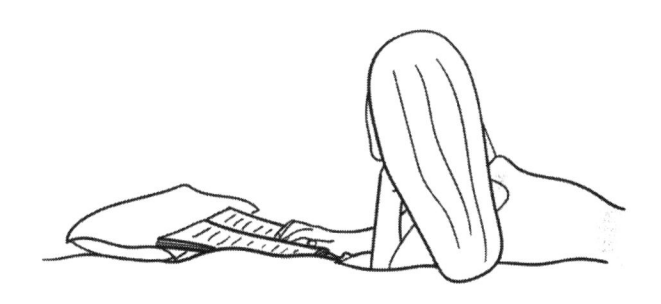

She is no ordinary woman.
You cannot overwhelm,
An ocean that separates oil.

She plays her hardships on an organ,
And serenades your presence.
Carrying both strength and duty,
To the heirs that made this race-

Omnificent.

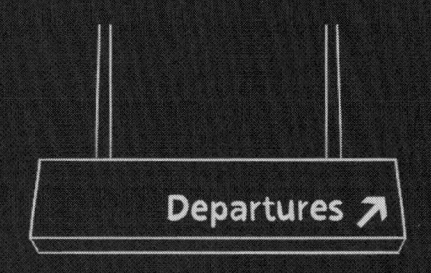

You continued to bless me,
even in your **departure**.

Mum

She was more than a mother,
More than a wife and a sister,
More than a friend,
More than a support system,
More than home.

She was everything,
She was ours.

Now I just miss
Your **embrace**.

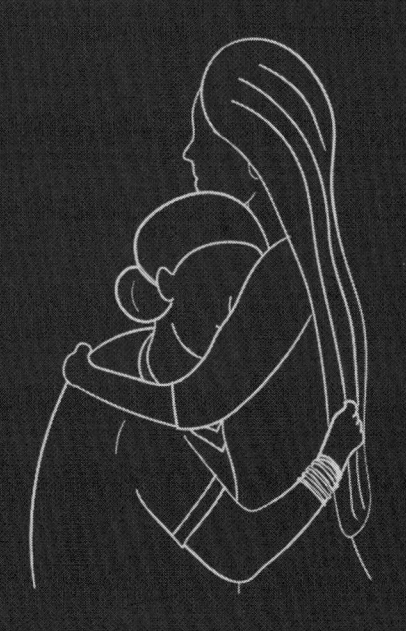

RECOVERY

Acknowledgments

I would like to say thank you, particularly to my family and friends who have supported me throughout the years, in putting my thoughts and emotions to paper. For always standing by me and for being the individuals in my life that I could share everything with.

A very special thank you to Satvir Sihota, the illustrator for my book. Your beautiful images brought lost memories to life. Thank you for making me feel like a real author.

To my lovely readers, you all bring such warmth, love and kindness into my life. Thank you for being a part of this journey with me, I would not be where I am today without you all.

Sending love, always
xxxxxx

RECOVERY

Dedications to my family

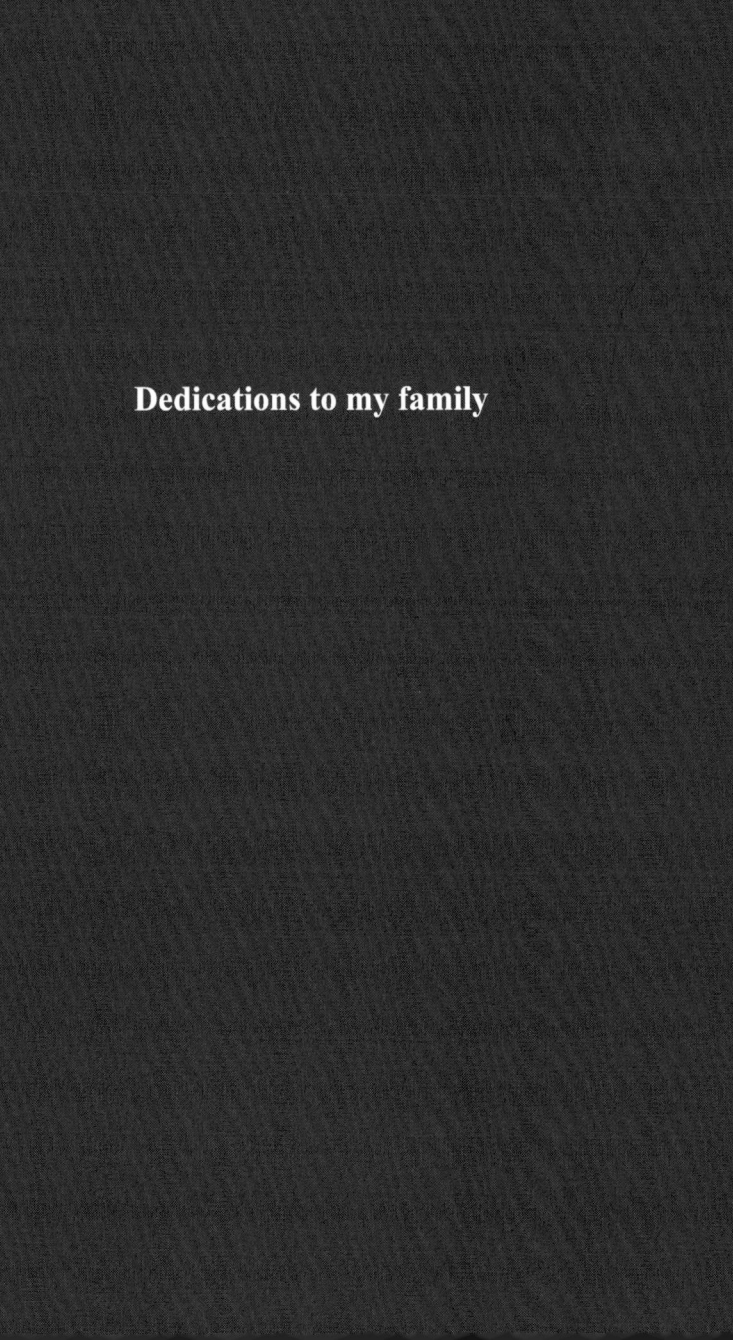

G.K.P

I lean on you, when I break.
You pick me up, always.

You raised me.

I seek your approval first, before the others.
I fear your disappointment, before the others.
I trust your judgment, better than mine.
You see things for me, when I turn blind.

I've always wanted to make my parents proud,
To show them, that I too can achieve great things.

But you are the person I look up to.
And I hope that one day,
I'll make you as proud, as I am of you.

H.P

You shield us from all things unpromising.
You hold on tight,
When things break loose.

You turn up,
When I call for you.
Your presence,
Is my security.

This brotherly love,
Is all that I could ask for.

N.K.S

You are my guideline, my calm, my clarity
You give me direction.

Your kindness shrinks darkness.
Your warmth keeps me from fear.
Your everything wraps around me,
As if I never lost anything.

H.S.S

Each time I've fallen,
You've been there to pick me up.

Your unspoken actions,
Blankets my fears.

Because I know, my big brother
Is always watching over me.

A.K.B

Your silence breaks the unbreakable.
Your laughter trembles unwanted fears.
You lift each room you walk into,
You lift me.

R.S.B

There has always been
An expectation I have
Set for myself.
To ensure I can achieve,
The things my father sees for me.

His boundless love and
Pride for his children,
Left a foundation to
Create a legacy.

S.S.B

If it's one thing I remember
About my grandfather,
It was his boldness.

His broad shoulders
Layered clothing
And warmness.

Your overworked hands,
Carried the weight
Of our family.

You taught us what
Love meant.

I love you Baba Ji.

RECOVERY

Ishpreet Kaur Bhogal, a 22 year old Punjabi Sikh writer and author from London, UK, turned to writing at the age of 15 to escape the harsh emotional and physical realities of caring for a loved one with cancer.

Creative writing has provided Ishpreet with a voice, a way to channel her thoughts and emotions through the traumatic and life-changing events she has encountered. By sharing her vulnerabilities through poetry, she aims to support others going through a similar journey.

Ishpreet's profound gratitude for her readers has only encouraged her to continue writing and she endeavours to share more on growth, relationships and self-discovery in the coming years.

This book is a dedication to Ishpreet's late mother, a testament to the unbreakable bond between mother and daughter.

@ishpreetwrites

Printed in Great Britain
by Amazon